# THE PREPPY GYRL DEVOTIONAL:

CAMPUS LIFE SCRIPTURES
AND DAILY LIVING
REFLECTIONS FOR
CHRISTIAN GIRLS IN
COLLEGE

# by LaToya N. Ausley

Copyright © 2017

by LaToya N. Ausley

All rights reserved. This book or any portion thereof may not be reproduced or used in any manner whatsoever without the express written permission of the publisher except for the use of brief quotations in a book review.

Printed in the United States of America

First Printing, 2017

ISBN 978 0 692 15690 2

Black Teen Girl Books & Bubblegum

www.preppygyrl.com

I dedicate this book back to God. For the girls of today that will become the ladies of tomorrow with distinction. Keep God first, stay submitted to the One True God and try your best to make wise decisions based on the Future You! With Love, Hunny Bunnies!

## Day 1

College is finally here hunny bunnies! As you embark on this new journey as a Christian girl in college, it is important that you keep God first in your actions and in your heart. The daily responsibilities of classes, study time, social activities and just finding the time to sleep can be challenging. So, of course, reading your Bible can become quite difficult to do during your college years. We understand that it isn't that you don't love God and have put Him on the shelf but rather, the pressures of college can be demanding and overwhelming.

The Preppy Gyrl Country Club Devotional for College Girls was created to help Christian girls in college maintain a devotional time with God, encourage discipline in searching the Bible for God's direction and provide real campus-life situations and challenges of daily living with scriptures as a resolution to a college girl's greatest struggles as a Christian on campus. The Devotional covers topics such as dating, pursuing love, choosing the appropriate friendships, depression, sex, drugs, alcohol, faith, atheism and unbelief, fashion etiquette, academic success and failure, discovering spiritual giftings, choosing a church home as a young adult and so much more.

Each daily entry has a supportive scripture in various versions of the Bible to assist in understanding the scriptures as well as encourage a hunger and thirst to become a student of the Word of God. Our prayer is that God will give you wisdom, knowledge and understanding as you enter this new season of adulthood! It is our prayer that you never lose your zeal for God! Have a wonderful college year!

**Psalms 63:1 NKJV**

Oh God, you are my God, early will I seek you. My soul thirsts for you. My flesh longs for you in a dry and thirsty land where there is no water.

**Day 2**

Life on campus can become very exciting. There are so many things to choose from that seem so much better than going to church, sitting in your dorm room reading your Bible and turning down parties, fine guys or sorority offers. However, the truth is, many of those things that are socially popular on campus are high risk for a Christian girl because the likelihood of it leading you into sin is very high. Do not be mesmerized at the dopeness of the college parties, the pretty girls in cute colors, drinking to look gorgeous and grown or sleeping in your boyfriend's room all of the time. These things and many more things that go on in the dorms and on campus can be appealing and fulfilling to your flesh. Life outside of it can seem so boring and even depressing. It is important that you choose your social interactions and activities wisely as a Christian girl in college.

That one shot that you take at the party could be spiked. The marijuana that you decide to try with your friends in your room could have other drugs mixed in it that causes the frontal lobe of your brain to be altered. The day that you decide to give up your virginity, you get pregnant or herpes. The one night that you take on the dare to kiss a girl in the room, you discover that you kind of like it and now you are struggling with whether you like girls or guys. Or, you decide to join that sorority and soon afterwards it is revealed that you just pledged your life to a Greek or Roman goddess.

So, you can afford to say "nah" to the things that seem like it is what's up. Do not let these things make you feel as though your life sucks as a Christian and you'd rather be at the party throwing up shots with your friends in your tight skimpy dress that has all the boys lookin. Do not desire this lifestyle more than the one that is pleasing to God. Do not let your fire for God go out. Do not let doing right become boring to you. Do not lose your excitement for the things that please God. Remember, being a Christian is not a punishment but a lifestyle to be admired.

**Romans 12:11-13 NIV**

11. Never be lacking in zeal but keep your spiritual ferver, serving the Lord. 12. Be joyful in hope, patient in affliction, faithful in prayer. 13. Share with the Lord's people who are in need, practice hospitality.

**Day 3**

Friendships are a blessing and are good for you. It is important that you take care of them as you would an intimate relationship. Strive to maintain those friendships that are important to you. Friendships are strong and healthy when you nurture them and give them the attention that they require. Don't neglect good friendships.

**Ecclesiastes 4:9-10 AMP**

Two are better than one because there is a more satisfying return for their labor. For if either of them fall, the one will lift up his companion but woe to him who is alone when he falls and does not have another to lift him up.

## Day 4

Be the kind of friend in someone else's life that you would like to have in your own life. Be open to new friendships and avoid being too stubborn about meeting new people.

### Proverbs 18:24 NKJV

A man that has friends must himself be friendly; but there is a friend that sticks closer than a brother.

**Day 5**

Choose your friends wisely. It is important that you choose friends with similar morals and values as yourself. The friendship will be stronger and positive for your continuous growth as a person.

**1 Corinthians 15:33 AMP**

Be not deceived, bad company corrupts good morals.

**Day 6**

Do you have faith? Faith is the foundation of our life as a Christian. Faith is having an unwavering trust in God. Exercise your faith in God today as you go through the day. Believe God and don't doubt. May your faith be increased today.

**1 Thessalonians 3:7**

For this reason, brothers and sisters, during all of our distress and suffering we have been comforted and greatly encouraged about you because of your faith; your unwavering trust in God, placing yourselves completely in his loving hands.

**Day 7**

Sometimes we can want something so bad that we will step outside of God's will to get it. Don't be afraid to wait. Is he really the one? Ask God and wait for the answer. Don't be so consumed about companionship that you miss out on how God is trying to prepare you for your future. A good and qualified boyfriend is just a small piece of the puzzle. Don't move too fast!

**Philippians 4:6 AMP**

Do not be anxious or worried about anything but in everything, every circumstance and situation by prayer and petition with thanksgiving, continue to make your specific requests known to God.

## Day 8

Don't let your mind wander on all of the bad things. There are times when our fears and worries can get the best of us. It can even cause us to fall into depression. Today, make every effort to replace every bad thought with a positive one. Defeat those depressing thoughts!

## Philippians 4:8 NKJV

Finally, brethren, whatever things are true, whatever things are noble, whatever things are just, whatever things are pure, whatever things are lovely, whatever things are of good report; if there is any virtue, if there is anything praise worthy, meditate (think) on these things.

**Day 9**

Why read horoscopes? That is Astrology. What is Astrology? It is the study of the movements and relative positions of celestial bodies interpreted as having an influence on human affairs in the natural world. What are celestial beings? These are things of the sky such as the sun, moon and stars. Do you believe that the sun, moon and stars have an influence on your life? As a Christian, we should trust God to direct us daily. It is as simple as reading a scripture a day about what concerns you about your life and asking the Holy Spirit to speak to you through the written word of God. Trust and rely on God to speak to you about your life everyday instead of the horoscopes. God will speak if you seek Him.

**Proverbs 3:5-7 AMP**

Trust in and rely confidently on the Lord with all your heart and do not rely on your own insight or understanding. 6. In all your ways know and acknowledge and recognize Him and He will make your path straight and smooth, removing obstacles that block your way. 7. Do not be wise in your own eyes. Fear the Lord with reverent awe and obedience and turn entirely away from evil.

## Day 10

It can be difficult to be nice to someone who has hurt or offended you, especially when they are really wrong. However, it is better for you to be kind and honest instead of trying to make them pay for how they hurt you. It is difficult at times but try your best to maintain and exemplify Godly character.

### Proverbs 3:3 AMP

Do not let mercy and kindness and truth leave you, instead let these qualities define you.

## Day 11

Good friends have disagreements. A friend that can tell you the truth is an awesome type of friendship. Honesty is a quality that you should look for in one that you call friend. No one wants a friend that will talk about them behind their back nor one that will smile in their face and not be honest. They are both harmful to you. If your friend has said something to you that hurts but you know that it is the truth, don't throw the friendship away because your feelings are hurt. Gather yourself and talk to your friend about how you feel about what they said to you. A good friend will not always say what feels good.

**Proverbs 27:6 NIV**

Wounds from a friend can be trusted but an enemy multiplies kisses.

## Day 12

What are your plans for your future? Do you have a major and career in mind? Do your parents have an expectation of who you will become? We have our ideas of what academic, career and even spiritual paths that we should take in our lives. The pressure can get overwhelming when we are trying to figure out our purpose. It can also be a heavy weight when we are trying to meet our parents' expectations of who we should become and what the path looks like to get there. Be thankful for parents and those around you that have instilled ideals of success in you. It gives you a starting point on what to pursue. However, God also has thoughts and plans for our lives. Pray and ask God what He wants you to do with your life. After you have prayed, pay attention to how your strengths will start to make more sense to you in the next couple of days. People around you will also start to mention your strengths and abilities to you without you asking. God has a plan for your life and He is concerned about your future.

**Proverbs 19:21 AMP**

Many plans are in a man's mind but it is the Lord's purpose for him that will stand and be carried out.

## Day 13

Being a Christian is not a punishment but a lifestyle to be admired. As a young Christian, it can sometimes seem as if you are missing out on something. It can seem like you are an outcast or considered the "Holy Girl". Your life and the way that you do things is not the same as those around you that are not Christians or those that are not living their lives as Christians. You must become comfortable with being different and standing out. It can be a struggle and quite tempting to avoid extreme partying, drinking and sensual dancing but you can do it! Remember, you have been set aside for God's purpose and your life is an example to others. The way that you act in front of others will either make them want to get to know your God or say no thanks. There is a blessing in being holy. Embrace who you are!

**Colossians 1:10 AMP**

So that you may walk in a manner worthy of the Lord, displaying admirable character, moral courage and personal integrity to fully please Him in all things; bearing fruit in every good work and steadily growing in the knowledge of God with deeper faith, clearer insight and fervent love for His precepts.

## Day 14

It can be hard to tell others about Christ. You don't want to sound like you are in church giving an altar call. You don't have to sound churchy. You can put things in your own words so that it is relatable and easy for your friends to understand. Introducing a friend to Christ is a rewarding experience. A friend that accepts Christ as their Lord and Savior is rewarding because you just helped to save a soul from hell. It is one of our main duties as Christians. Take your time and make sure that you are ready and confident to introduce others to Christ. You can prepare yourself by knowing God's Word and what He says about how people get saved, why and its importance. As you understand this scripture for yourself, you will gain confidence to share it with others. Today's scripture is what you need to study and know to offer salvation to others. What is the next step? We will talk about it tomorrow. Have a wonderful day today and shine bright in your own way!

## Romans 10:8-14 AMP

"[Saved by our own efforts, doing the impossible]." 8 But what does it say? "The word is near you, in your mouth and in your heart"—that is, the word [the message, the basis] of faith which we preach— 9 because if you acknowledge and confess with your mouth that Jesus is Lord [recognizing His power, authority, and majesty as God], and believe in your heart that God raised Him from the dead, you will be saved. 10 For with the heart a person believes [in Christ as Savior] resulting in his justification [that is, being made righteous—being freed of the guilt of sin and made acceptable to God]; and with the mouth he acknowledges and confesses [his faith openly], resulting in and confirming [his] salvation. 11 For the Scripture says, "Whoever believes in Him [whoever adheres to, trusts in, and relies on Him] will not be disappointed [in his expectations]." 12 For there is no distinction between Jew and Gentile; for the same Lord is Lord over all [of us], and [He is] abounding in riches (blessings) for all who call on Him [in faith and prayer]. 13 For "whoever calls on the name of the Lord [in prayer] will be saved." 14 But how will people call on Him in whom they have not believed? And how will they believe in Him of whom they have not heard? And how will they hear without a preacher.

## Day 15

Now that you have the scriptures to help you to introduce others to Christ; what do you do now? It is important that you invite them to your church or direct them to one that you think would be good for them. It is time for them to learn more about God and what it means to be a Christian. It is important that they not only accept Christ but they must also be instructed and in an environment to help them grow as a Christian. Faith comes by hearing and hearing comes by the Word of God. One of the ways that they can hear the Word of God is through a preacher. The preacher has been authorized by God to teach, watch over our souls and pray for us often.

**Romans 10:14 AMP**

But how will they call on Him in whom they have not believed and how will they believe in Him whom they have not heard and how will they hear without a preacher (messenger)?

## Day 16

Who has hurt you? There are times in our lives when people do things that hurt us intentionally and even unintentionally. It can hurt so bad that we just don't want to forgive them and it is hard to just let it go and act like it never happened. In times like these, it is important that you do not hold unforgiveness in your heart towards those that hurt you because it can cause you to become bitter and even hold grudges. Bitterness is anger and disappointment at being treated unfairly; resentment. Resentment is bitter indignation at having been treated unfairly. Here is the key part of bitterness and resentment that makes things go really bad. It's called indignation, which is when you are provoked to anger because of your bitterness. Furthermore, indignation is also to regard as unworthy. If something or someone is unworthy to you, the next thing that you will see come out of your heart, mind and mouth is disrespect towards that person. As you can see, while the beginning of bitterness is someone hurting you, if you let those feelings of hurt and pain stay there and pile up, it creates you to be the monster. The pretty girl with the nasty attitude, hard heart, foul mouth and oh so disrespectful; all the time. Ask God to help you to really forgive those that hurt you and the side effects of bitterness to be removed from you. Your job is to monitor your character and behavior so that you don't become the pretty girl monster. Hard hearts are insensitive. Hard hearts don't feel, just like monsters. Talk to God about your hurts and disappointments, monitor your behavior, words and inner thoughts and once you get to a peaceful place, try to talk to the person that hurt you about how they hurt you, if possible. However, this is not always possible or healthy. In circumstances where you should not or are just not in a good place to talk to the person that hurt you, keep talking to God about it daily. Be honest with God and He will begin to soften your heart.

**Ephesians 4:27 AMP**

And do not give the devil an opportunity to lead you into sin by holding a grudge or nurturing anger or harboring resentment or cultivating bitterness.

## Day 17

Grudge - a persistent feeling of ill will or resentment resulting from a past injury or insult.

Who are you holding a grudge against? It is easy to keep holding it because you feel entitled. You feel like you deserve to feel like you do and you are probably right. Yes, you were hurt by that person but you can't keep holding on to what happened in the past. It is time for you to let it go for your own peace of mind, to regain a softened heart and to stay out of sin. Harboring, holding and cultivating are all acts done by you and are in your control to stop or continue. Yes, it is difficult to quickly change our feelings toward people that have done us wrong. Your goal is to start to replace your ill feelings with kind thoughts and actions every time that you encounter them. It is a process and it will take time but keep thinking good thoughts and they will lead to good actions.

**Ephesians 4:27 AMP**

And do not give the devil an opportunity to lead you into sin by holding a grudge or harboring resentment or cultivating bitterness.

## Day 18

"We love to party! We love to dance! What is the big deal with me going to a party as a Christian?"

As a Christian, it is important that you monitor the environments that you put yourself in, the people that you choose to hang around and what you hear and see. So, you're at the party and they are just dancing. There's no harm in that. Right? Dancing does not become an issue until it becomes sensual; meaning of a sexual nature. We all know that at most high school, college and even junior high schools, more than likely there is grinding, humping or close contact to receive some kind of sexual pleasure. Even if you dance alone, if the music and environment are of that nature, it will ignite a sexual passion, thought or urge. It is all about your thoughts. Party environments with dancing are for sure places to get your sexual desires and thoughts stirred. As a Christian, you must monitor how much of this you participate in to maintain pure thoughts and avoid temptations. No one wants to live a boring life as a young Christian but you have been set apart for God's purpose and because of this, there are things that you just can't do. You must actively watch for things that can entrap you. For ladies, sexual desires and urges start in the mind and are usually provoked by music, close dancing, soft caresses and charming guys that can make you blush and your heart melt. Dancing is never just dancing in your case. It is a trap that will get you longing for something that you should not have, which is sex. Enjoy the party but watch how far you go. If you can't control yourself and maintain purity in your words, actions and thoughts, Do Not Go to the party!

### Ephesians 4:19-23 AMP

19 And they, [the ungodly in their spiritual apathy], having become callous and unfeeling, have given themselves over [as prey] to unbridled sensuality, eagerly craving the practice of every kind of impurity [that

their desires may demand]. 20 But you did not learn Christ in this way! 21 If in fact you have [really] heard Him and have been taught by Him, just as truth is in Jesus [revealed in His life and personified in Him], 22 that, regarding your previous way of life, you put off your old self [completely discard your former nature], which is being corrupted through deceitful desires, 23 and be continually renewed in the spirit of your mind [having a fresh, untarnished mental and spiritual attitude]

**Day 19**

True friendship is... saying that I miss you as my friend. A broken friendship can be restored if both parties are willing to set their pride aside. It hurts to lose a good friend, especially when you know that you stopped being friends over something stupid. In cases like these, someone has to be the bigger person. This is a great example of how beneficial it is to have a Christian friend. There may be animosity between you all and you may not even be talking to one another but if both of you are willing to forgive and talk about your hurts, the friendship can get better. Don't let animosity sit on your heart toward your friends. Express yourself to them in a kind way. Don't snap off even though you may be hurt. Prepare yourself through prayer to put your guard down. Animosity towards someone is a big fight on the inside of you. It is a strong feeling of hostility. What does it mean to be hostile? It is to be unfriendly and antagonistic. What is antagonistic? It is showing active opposition or hostility towards someone or something. So, what does that active opposition really mean? This type of opposition is like an adversary/enemy, rival or competitor. Animosity is a feeling but is shown through hostility towards the one that you see as your enemy. So, is the one that 're not talking to, an enemy or friend? Think about this really hard and evaluate the pros and cons of how that person has been as a friend. Once you have it all laid out; is it worth it? A good friend is worth fighting for when you know that they have been a good friend. Forgive and be vulnerable enough to ask for forgiveness.

**Ephesians 4:31-32 AMP**

30. Let all bitterness and wrath and anger and clamour; perpetual animosity, resentment, strife, fault finding and slander be put away from you along with every kind of malice, all spitefulness, verbal abuse, malevolence. 32. Be kind and helpful to one another, tender-hearted, compassionate,

understanding, forgiving one another readily and freely just as God in Christ also forgave you.

## Day 20

"Ooh! She made me so mad!! I had to curse her out!"

Have you ever said these words? Sometimes when others make us angry, it is so easy for us to use our words to hurt them. Then, there are times when we curse because it makes us sound cool or tough. You're grown. You can say what you want, right? Ok, or maybe your cursing is just a bad habit. It's so hard to stop. Everybody around you curses all the time. What is the big deal? They are just words. Let us see what a curse actually means. According to the Oxford Dictionary, a curse is an offensive word or phrase to express anger or annoyance.

As we can see, usually curse words come out when we are either angry or annoyed. However, these feelings do not give us the right to curse, as Christians. We must try our best to exercise self control. Today, when you get annoyed or angry, pay close attention to the words that you speak. The more that you can control your mouth, the less that you will find the need to use curse words to express yourself.

**Ephesians 4:29 AMP**

Do not let unwholesome, foul, profane, worthless vulgar words ever come out of your mouth but only such as is good for building up others according to the need and occasion so that it may be a blessing to those that hear you speak.

## Day 21

Let's talk more about those words mentioned yesterday in Ephesians 4:29. Are your curse words falling into the category of being considered foul, unwholesome, profane or vulgar? Let's take a look. To be profane is a person or their behavior not showing respect for orthodox religious practices; irreverent, of language blasphemous or obscene. How about being vulgar? What is that? Vulgar is to lack sophistication or good taste; to be coarse, rude and obscene and use explicit references to sex or bodily functions. Does this sound Christ-like yet? Let's take a quick look at one more word that the Bible describes as a type of word that should not come out of our mouths. So, are you being foul when you curse? Foul is of a language that is obscene or profane. Hmmm... Are your words unwholesome? Take the time today to express your feelings without using foul, profane and vulgar words. These are not always feelings of anger or annoyance that cause us to curse. Often, people will curse when they are excited, happy, emphasizing or just because but you must not use these as reasons to curse. Monitor your words and how you choose to express yourself. It will get better each day that you try!

## Day 22

"What is it like to live my life as a Christian? It seems like there are so many things that I can't do. My life would be so boring if I really tried to live like a Christian."

This could very well be true. As such, this is why it is important to have some friends that believe what you believe and are striving to live a lifestyle that is pleasing to God. If you have these kinds of friends around you, it can be very helpful. As friends, you all will be an encouragement to each other to continue to do the right things as opposed to feeling like the odd-ball and being pressured by your own thoughts or others' words to do things that you shouldn't. It is so vital to have Christian friends around you that are excited about God and growing as Christians. You will find that you will start to enjoy the things of God. Hearing God confirm things in your life, provide you with direction for your future, receiving prophetic words from the Lord, attending praise and worship events and conferences will soon become fun and exciting to you. Living a Christian lifestyle is difficult as a young adult when there are so many things in this world to tempt you. A good friend will keep you accountable and help you stay on track and you will be able to do the same for them.

**Ephesians 4:1 AMP**

So I, the prisoner for the Lord, appeal to you to live a life worthy of the calling to which you have been called. That is, to live a life that exhibits Godly character, moral courage, personal integrity and mature behavior. A life that expresses gratitude to God for your salvation.

**Day 23**

Who are you not talking to at this time? Do you have a problem with someone? Is it worrying you, stressing you out, and you have no peace? This is a tough one today! So, who is going to be the peacemaker in that situation that you are in with that person that you care about? I think that you already know who and why!

**Ephesians 4:3 AMP**

Make every effort to keep the oneness of the Spirit and the bond of peace; each individual working to make the whole successful.

## Day 24

There are some people that can really get on your nerves. They can get under your skin so bad that it will make you want to scream. If you get to points like these in your emotions, you must stop and gain some self control. It is important that you try your best to not let people take you out of character. It's difficult to love someone like this, isn't it? However, we must try to love them with a God type of love, it is an unselfish love. We may think that they don't deserve our kindness but it is something that we should do as Christians. It is humbling and it can really hurt our flesh to be nice and gentle to someone that really gets on our nerves or has upset or disappointed us. Try, try, try to find a way to be kind and get some control over your emotions. Warning, it will start with you humbling yourself.

**Ephesians 4:2 AMP**

With all humility, forsaking self-righteousness and gentleness, maintaining self control with patience, bearing with one another in unselfish love (agape love).

## Day 25

So what! I mean, what if I don't follow all of this stuff in the Bible? I don't think that it will hurt anyone. There are people in the world doing worse things than me. My little sins are not that bad anyway. God is not that affected if I don't do the things that please Him, right?

## Ephesians 4:30 AMP

And do not grieve the Holy Spirit of God but seek to please Him by whom you were sealed, marked as God's own for the day of redemption; the final deliverance for the consequences of sin.

## Day 26

There is a blessing in obeying God's word. It is important that we humble ourselves before our Father by being honest with Him about all of our feelings, good and bad. A repentant spirit gets God's attention. You don't have to run and hide from our God because you feel bad about something that you have done. The key thing about repentance is that when you ask God for forgiveness, you must mean it. To ask God to forgive you is not just you saying I am sorry but turning away from the thing that you did. You can't keep doing it and asking God to forgive you afterwards. Try to always have a repentant heart even if you are still trying to get rid of some sins. Remember, to be repentant is to turn away from it and not do it again.

**Isaiah 66:2 AMP**

For all these things my hand has made so all these things came into being by and for me, declares the Lord. But to this one I will look graciously; to him who is humble and contrite in spirit and who reverently trembles at my word and honors my commands.

## Day 27

Many may try to debate with you about what you believe. Do you know where God's throne is? It is important that you are able to find it in the Bible for yourself. It will give you confidence!

### Isaiah 66:1 AMP

This is what the Lord says, Heaven is my throne and the earth is my footstool. Where, then is a house that you could build for me and where will my resting place be?

## Day 28

Have you ever heard someone say that they are not sure where this world came from? In college classes, especially Science and Philosophy, you may be challenged with this question. Did God create the heavens and the earth? How do you know? Are you ready for someone to ask you this and have a confident answer?

### Isaiah 66:1-2 AMP

1.This is what the Lord says, heaven is my throne and the earth is my footstool. Where, then is a house that you could build for me and where will my resting place be? 2.For all these things my hand has made; so all these things came

into being, by and for me,
declares the Lord...

## Day 29

Do you have a best friend? Have you thought about why you consider her your best friend? A good friend is genuine and only wants what is best for you. They should be able to tell you the truth, even if it hurts. A good friend will not watch you fall and not warn you if she sees it coming. A real friend protects you from harm, humiliation and gossip. She will want to see you succeed and not do sneaky things to secretly hope that you fail. Your friends should be a safe place. A place where you can trust them with the things of your heart. Sometimes, we call people friends that have not shown or no longer show themselves as friends. It doesn't matter how long you've been friends. It is more important for you to know that it is a quality friendship. Quality over quantity!

**Proverbs 27:9 AMP**

Oil and perfume make the heart glad, so does the sweetness of a friend's counsel that comes from the heart.

## Day 30

Has anyone challenged you about why you are a Christian? Are they holding a strong opinion that there is no God? Let's be real! Why are you believing in some God that you can't see? Do you have a response for them?

### John 20:29-31 AMP

29. Jesus said to him, because you have seen me, now do you believe? Blessed, happy, spiritually secure and favored by God are they that did not see me and yet believed in me.
30. There are also many other signs; attesting miracles, that Jesus performed in the presence of the disciples which are not written in this book.
31. But these have been

written so that you may believe with a deep abiding trust that Jesus is the Christ, the Messiah, the Anointed, the Son of God and that by believing and trusting and relying on Him, you may have life in His name.

## Day 31

"Why are you reading the Bible? It's just a book. It's all made up stories in it. It's like Greek mythology or something."

Have you heard these statements in your Philosophy, English Literature or Humanities classes on campus? Do you know why you believe what's in the Bible? What's the point? The Bible is the inspired words of God, whether He spoke directly or inspired other men and women to speak and record their journeys or moments that God deemed significant. If you are a Christian you believe in God and you trust in Him; His words, principles, revelation of who He is, His ways, what He thinks and feels about certain things and so much more are all written in the Holy Bible that we consider to be sacred and important to our lives.

## 2 Timothy 3:16 AMP

All scripture is God breathed, given by divine inspiration and is profitable for instruction, for conviction of sin, for correction of error and restoration to obedience, for training in righteousness; learning to live in conformity to God's will both publicly and privately; behaving honorably with personal integrity and moral courage.

**Day 32**

"How do I pray? I really have a hard time with praying. Is God really listening? I just don't know what to say. I feel like I am talking to the air."

**Proverbs 15:29 AMP**

The Lord is far from the wicked and distances himself from them but He hears the prayer of the consistently righteous, that is, those with spiritual integrity and moral courage.

## Day 33

There are so many people on your campus and many of them are of different religions. Each of them have a belief about their god, worship practices and foundational principles. Do you treat them wrong and mean because they don't believe the same as you? Absolutely not! It is important that you understand your religious beliefs and its foundation so that you are not persuaded by the religious debates that may come from your friends of different religious, cultural or ethnic backgrounds. Sometimes, popular culture can also be very influential in proposing new ways of living and beliefs that are not consistent with your beliefs. You may receive some scrutiny for what you believe and some may even say that it's stupid. However, it doesn't matter what others are saying or doing, it is vital that you are confident in your beliefs. If not, you will be easily persuaded and could ignorantly change religions or come home from college professing that you don't believe in God anymore. As Christians, the foundation of all that we believe is faith. It is a deep, unwavering trust in God, The Most High, not buddha, Allah or any other false god. We believe that there is only one true God.

**Hebrews 11:6 AMP**

But without faith it is impossible to walk with God and please Him, for whoever comes near to God must necessarily believe that God exists and that He rewards those who earnestly and diligently seek Him.

## Day 34

"Man, I really messed up last night! I knew that I shouldn't have done that! I just couldn't control myself. I really tried to stop. I know that God is mad at me. I feel horrible! Is God going to forgive me for this one?"

### 1 John 1:9 AMP

If we freely admit that we have sinned and confess our sins. He is faithful and just, true to His own nature and promises and will forgive our sins and cleanse us continually from all unrighteousness, our wrongdoing, everything not in conformity with His will and purpose.

## Day 35

"I am really trying to be right. I don't sin like these other girls on campus. They have sex with a bunch of guys, go to parties and get drunk and everything. I don't do any of those things."

Of course, while these sins may not be your particular issue, there are still sins that we have committed that are not always as obvious and external. No one is perfect and sin-free. It is important that we always admit that we have sinned and there is something about us that we can improve and is probably considered to be sin according to the Bible. We are not perfect but we serve a God that is a forgiving God.

**1 John 1:10 AMP**

If we say that we have not sinned, refusing to admit acts of sin, we make Him out to be a liar by contradicting Him and His word is not in us.

## Day 36

Social media can boost confidence and at other times, it can make you feel not so confident and even unpopular. It is quite easy to gain confidence from numerous likes, comments and followers on social media platforms. However, what about when you don't get many likes and comments on your posts? How about when you don't have as many followers as her? Do you still feel confident about yourself, your beauty or intellect? It is important that you don't allow likes, comments or followers to define you.

You should maintain positive thoughts about yourself regardless of responses on social media. It can be tough to look at others and it seems like they are so popular. Maybe, you're thinking, "What does she have that I don't? She's always showing everything on her selfies. Am I not pretty enough? Maybe I should unbutton my shirt a little more on my next pic? Maybe I should turn to the side a little so that my curve on my booty can show? I got to show something! Right?"

It is a blessing to be beautiful and have a nice body but it should not be the only thing that you have as an asset. It is just as important that you have an inner beauty adorned with great character, modesty, high morals, standards and behavior that reflect a young lady that's submitted to living a clean and pure lifestyle. A beautiful heart and spirit is pleasing to God and attractive to a good guy. Good guys look at your outward beauty, of course! However, he sticks around based on your inner beauty. So, you need both, not just a pretty face and a nice body! It is ok to keep a modest image on social media. It will attract the right guys and friends that are just right for you!

### 1 Peter 3:3-4 AMP

3. Your adornment must not be merely external with interweaving and elaborate

knotting of the hair and wearing gold jewelry or being superficially pre-occupied with wearing expensive clothes. 4. But let it be the inner beauty, the hidden person of the heart with the imperishable quality and unfading charm of a gentle and peaceful spirit; one that is calm and self-controlled not over anxious but is serene and spiritually mature which is very precious in the sight of God.

## Day 37

There are many ways to pray to God. It really depends on your personality and the type of relationship that you feel that you have with God. Do you see him as a father, friend, Lord or something else? Do you pray very formal and religious? Do you say the same prayer over and over again everyday? Is your heart not in it and there's really no meaning to it? Are you an on the go type of prayer girl? Do you pray as you are moving around and getting dressed in the morning? Are you the type of prayer girl that talks to God about everything and you do it all day as often as you feel the need to do so? None of these are wrong and as you learn more about God and mature in your understanding of who God is, your prayer language will change as well. Jesus does provide a framework on how we should pray. This does not mean repeating the words exactly that He mentions but rather covering the basics in your prayers as you pray. The framework is the Lord's Prayer but this does not mean that you have to say it word for word. Your prayers should always include acknowledgment of who God is, praise to His name, request that His will be done in you and on earth, request that God gives you what you will need to have a fruitful and pleasing day to Him, forgive others, ask God for forgiveness of your sins, ask to be delivered from evil which is protection, ask to be guided by God so that you are not lead into temptation and more praise to His name is always acceptable. The rest of your prayer has in it your more personal requests, whatever they may be along with prayer for others. Don't feel like you have to sound like a certain person or do prayer like them. Just be sure to cover the basics and add on everything else that you have to say to God. All can be done in your own words and with your personal style. May you be free to talk to God in your own way and gain confidence during your prayer time. The best way to get to know God is to read His Holy Word, the Holy Bible.

**Matthew 6:6-13 AMP**

6. But when you pray, go into your most private room, close the door and pray to your Father who is in secret and your Father who sees what is done will reward you. 7. And when you pray, do not use meaningless repetitions as the gentiles do for they think that they will be heard because of their many words. 8. So do not be like them, praying as they do. For your Father knows what you need before you ask Him. 9. Pray, then, in this way; Our Father who is in heaven, hallowed be your name. 10. Your kingdom come, your will be done on earth as it is in heaven. 11. Give us this day our daily bread. 12. And forgive us our debts as we

have forgiven our debtors;
letting go of both the wrong
and the resentment. 13. And
do not lead us into temptation
but deliver us from evil. For
yours is the kingdom and the
power and the glory forever.
Amen

## Day 38

One of the best ways to get to know God, recognize Him and His ways is to read God's Holy Word, the Holy Bible. Ask God for understanding before you read and invite the Holy Spirit in to be with you as you study the Bible. Quality time is required with God to get to know Him. There are no shortcuts! Take the time to study the Bible just like you would do for your classes on campus. It's just as important.

2 Timothy 2:7 AMP

Think over the things I am saying, grasp their application, for the Lord will give you insight and understanding in everything.

## Day 39

There are some things that are going to be difficult to manage while you are living on campus. It can be challenging to avoid staying over your boyfriend's house or dorm room overnight. However, this is a sin trap waiting to happen. It is important that you pay close attention to your passionate desires and manage them well. This means that when you are feeling weak and passionate, you must avoid situations that will allow you to fulfill your lusts. You must stay out of his room when you are feeling weak.

### 2 Timothy 2:22 AMP

Run away from youthful lusts. Pursue righteousness, faith,

love and peace with those believers who call on the Lord out of a pure heart.

**Day 40**

To delight means to take great pleasure in. Do you find joy and fulfillment in reading your Bible and getting to know who God is? Do you enjoy times of prayer and worship to God? Do you get excited about going to church on Sundays? Do you find yourself sitting on the edge of your seat in church because you are excited about what God is about to say? There is a blessing in taking pleasure in the things of God. Take some time today to think about what you enjoy about being a Christian. It is important that you love and enjoy spending time with the God that you serve.

**Psalms 37:4 AMP**

Delight yourself in the Lord and He will give you the desires and petitions of your heart.

## Day 41

Dedicate your life and all that it entails to God. In order to do this, you must also trust Him. Do you trust God? Do you believe that He has good plans for you and knows what's best for you? If you can't say at this time that you trust God, take some time to think about why you don't trust God. Once you have an answer, talk to God about it and be honest. During your most vulnerable and honest moments to God, you will start to experience God's peace, comfort and assurance of the blessings and benefits of trusting in Him. Try to be willing and open to dedicating areas of your life to God that you normally wouldn't today.

Think about these things as you walk to your next class!

**Psalms 37:5 AMP**

Commit your way to the Lord, trust in Him also and He will do it.

**Day 42**

Did you think more about if you are committing your life to God and trusting in Him? To trust God is to rely on and have confidence in Him. Trust is built in any relationship over time with results of being a safe place to entrust. May God show you today that you can trust Him!

**Psalms 37:3 AMP**

Trust, rely on and have confidence in the Lord and do good. Dwell in the land and feed securely on His faithfulness.

## Day 43

There are many that have gifts given to them by Jesus. As you mature and learn more about God along with recognizing his presence; you will start to notice many of the spiritual gifts within you. These gifts are given by God to His people in order to teach and build up the saints so that they may be able to go out into the world and serve people, that is, do ministry. If we are taught how to do ministry, it reproduces people and leaders that are gifted by Jesus and as a result, we have more equipped leaders to assist in helping God's people and bringing more people into the kingdom of God. There are some people that are destined to be leaders in the church. Are you starting to notice that God is calling you to be a leader in the church? Pay close attention to how you interact with your friends on campus and how the Holy Spirit speaks to you when you are around them. Do you find yourself wanting to teach them? Do you find yourself wanting to correct them? Do you often get information about people in your dreams or while you are awake and it happens? Do your friends look to you for advice on decisions that they need to make? Are you the final decision maker in the crew? Are you always telling people about God or feeling like their life would be better if they got to know more about Jesus and went to church?

Girl, God may be calling you to be a leader in His church! Pray and ask the Lord to show you the gifts that He has placed inside of you.

### Ephesians 4:11-12 AMP

11. And His gifts to the church were varied and He Himself appointed some as apostles - special messengers/representatives, some as prophets - who speak a new message from God to the people, some as evangelists - who spread the good news of salvation and some as pastors and teachers - to Shepard, guide and instruct. 12. And He did this to fully equip and perfect the saints (God's people) for works of service to

build up the Body of Christ -
the church.

## Day 44

"It is so busy today! I am running late for class! I need to print this paper out! I need to curl my hair, hop in the shower and do my makeup! I need to hurry up!"

During this time of rushing, you quickly say, "thank you Lord for this day!" These type of days happen often when you are living on campus or even commuting to college. However, it is important that you set your alarm early enough to pray without rushing, read a scripture that you can get some understanding on which will only come from spending time with God and waiting for God to speak to you about your day. This is a tough one to do when your life is so busy. It requires discipline and an adjustment in your lifestyle but it is rewarding. You will be more calm, focused, confident and fulfilled. What a blessing it is to have taken the time to talk to God, share your heart and concerns, express your gratefulness and through that, God spoke back to you. To top it off, you now have a scripture that you can understand and think about throughout your day. If things remain good or start to frustrate you, you'll have that scripture in your heart to encourage you to overcome the adversity. Prayer and spending quality time with God is important and essential to building a good relationship with the Lord. Be careful of having too many rushed mornings.

**Colossians 4:2 AMP**

Be persistent and devoted to prayer, being alert and focused in your prayer life with an attitude of Thanksgiving.

## Day 45

Rumors! Rumors! Rumors! Are you the one spreading them or are you the one that the rumor is about? A rumor is a currently circulating story or report of uncertain or doubtful truth. It is clear that we should not spread rumors about people. That lesson was learned in elementary school. Now, what about when you spread a rumor about yourself? How can this be? Let's say that you had a Psychology exam last week and you received a high B but when your classmates asked you what got on the exam, you told them that you received an A. Ironically, the word starts to circulate around the class that you received an A on the exam.

However, they never ask if they can see your paper but what if someone does? What will you do? What will you say to defend yourself? We are not in control of the information that others share about us. A rumor is not necessarily always a bad story that is circulating. It can also be good things. The reason that the story is considered a rumor is because it is unverified information. Be careful of lying about things about yourself that can quickly become rumors.

**Ephesians 4:25 AMP**

Therefore, rejecting all falsehood whether lying, defrauding, telling half-truths, spreading rumors; any such as

these, speak truth each one
with his neighbor for we are all
parts of one another and we
are all parts of the Body of
Christ.

## Day 46

I decided to accept Jesus into my life as my Lord and Savior but I still think about some of those old things that I would do. I want to do better and live like a Christian but it's hard and it's boring. Yes, everyday it is a challenge to live like a Christian when there are so many options and temptations in the world. It is a decision on a daily basis to not do the things that we would do in our past. The decision starts in your heart and mind. A fresh attitude about the new you will give you strength to do something new regarding your daily living.

**Ephesians 4:23 AMP**

And be continually renewed in the spirit of your mind, having a fresh, untarnished mental and spiritual attitude.

## Day 47

"I don't like this major anymore. I just don't think it is for me. My classes in my major are getting too hard and it is taking up a lot of my time. I have to study so many hours! My friends don't have to study this much in their major. I should just change my major. I mean, I can major in something else and still get a good job. Right? Um, this is hard! Should I change this major? Ugh, I want to, but I feel like something is telling me not to do it. This is a lot for me."

Yes, you will be faced with many decisions that you will have to make in college, some of them will be major life changing decisions while others may seem minor. Regardless of the type of decision that you are facing, it is important that you ask God to give you wisdom and clarity so that you can make a good decision. One that will keep you on the right path for your future. Choosing majors can be tricky but there is a major with a career connected to it that is just right for you. Don't run because your classes are getting hard. May God show you your strengths today so that you can use wisdom to choose the major that is just right for you and your future!

**James 1:5 AMP**

If any of you lacks wisdom to guide him through a decision

or circumstance, he is to ask
of our benevolent God who
gives to everyone generously
and without rebuke or blame
and it will be given to him.

## Day 48

Are you still having a hard time with that decision? Did you pray and you think that you heard God answer? However, you are not totally sure if you are hearing correctly. This is a major decision and I have to make a choice today, are your thoughts! In times like these, it is always best to have someone that you can call on for help. The key is to go to someone that will give you Godly and wise advice. They should give you God's perspective on the matter and any wisdom, usually from experience, that they can provide you. You do not have to make that decision alone. There is safety in Christ-centered counsel.

**Proverbs 11:14 NKJV**

Where there is no counsel, the people fall but in the multitude of counselors, there is safety.

**Day 49**

**Hebrews 10:36 AMP**

For you have need of patient endurance to bear up under difficult circumstances without compromising so that when you have carried out the will of God, you may receive and enjoy to the full what is promised.

## Day 50

AKA pledge and the blatant contradiction to the Holy Bible is provided below. Are you considering pledging to a sorority? Yes, the colors are pretty, the community service is great, the connections can be beneficial to your potential career and Ooh, those parties and the reputation of being known as a Pretty and Smart girl! It is quite fitting for a good girl! Right? Well, maybe not so much when it requires you, as a Christian to pledge your heart, mind and strength to another god. Let's take the blindfolds off of you and show you why you shouldn't join a sorority. It is very simple. Check it out!

### The AKA Pledge

To thee o Alpha Kappa Alpha, we pledge our hearts, our minds, our strength to foster thy teachings, obey thy laws and make thee supreme and service to all mankind. O Alpha Kappa Alpha, we greet thee.

Scriptures on what God says about what was said in the pledge:

**Deuteronomy 6:5-6**

**Matthew 22:37**

**Mark 12:30**

**Luke 10:27**

This is the greatest commandment given in the Bible.

\* There is an idol in your heart and you put it there by the words that you spoke. There can only be one supreme. In this pledge, AKA is the false god. There are indicators by the usage of words like thee, thy and supreme. There is also reference to thy teachings and thy laws. These are religious words and AKA is being referenced as a being as opposed to an organization. In addition, at the end of the pledge, the statement is made that " O AKA, we greet thee." This is acknowledging the presence of something. What is that something that you are acknowledging? This pledge is said at every meeting and is private. Who are you greeting when you say this at the end? You may want to say that AKA is not a false god but the proof is in the pledge. The use of words like thee and thy are words that elude to sacred or holy.

If that is not enough, the use of the word supreme being referenced to AKA places it in a high place. There can only be one supreme and that is the almighty God and beside Him, there is no other. We should not allow any other to take God's place. There is no room for two. You should not have any other gods before the one true God. To acknowledge something else as supreme is doing just that. You are placing it higher than the one true God. To be supreme means that it is superior to all others. If you are AKA, The fact that you profess these words out of your mouth often, you are professing that AKA stands in a superior place in your life, particularly in your heart, mind and strength which are areas that should be dedicated to the one true God, our Father in Heaven.

What about those teachings and laws mentioned in the pledge that are being professed? Doesn't that sound religious in nature? Teachings in law? Doesn't that sound similar to the Bible and how we reference it as the law and its teachings? These are words that define doctrine, which are a set of beliefs taught by a church or organization. The word doctrine derives from Latin, meaning teaching, learning and teach.

In totality, the pledge that you are saying is professing that you pledge to make thee supreme, in this pledge, the thee is the being, AKA. This sounds like you are a part of another religion and you have professed it out of your mouth. So, you can't be Christian and Greek. You must renounce one of them! That false God has to go and if you haven't pledged yet, don't do it! Do not let that idol in! You can only be deceived when you don't have knowledge to defend what is being presented to you. The blindfold is off!

Idol- an image or representation of a god used as an object of worship.

Renounce- refuse to abide by or recognize any longer.

**Deuteronomy 6:5-6 AMP**

5. You should love the Lord thy God with all your heart and mind and with all your soul and with all your strength; your entire being. 6. These words which I am commanding you today shall be written on your heart and mind.

**Matthew 22:37-38 AMP**

37. And Jesus replied to him, you should love the Lord your God with all your heart and with all your soul and with all

your mind. 38. This is the first and greatest commandment.

## Day 51

Good morning! Did you know that God loves you? Yes, God loves you! You are the apple of His eye. Keep this in your heart and mind as you go to class and move around your college campus today! God is love!

### 1 John 4:16 AMP

We have come to know by personal observation and experience and have believed with deep, consistent faith the love that God has for us. For God is love and the one who abides in love, abides in God and God abides continually in him.

**Day 52**

There are times when you may wonder, "Why do I have to go through this?" You may say, "Why won't this problem go away?" God has given you grace for that situation. What is grace? It is to be in God's unmerited favor. It is not something that you have done to deserve it. So, no matter the weaknesses that that you may see in yourself or the difficult situations that may be going on in your life, God's grace is enough to put you at ease. You are favored by God.

**2 Corinthians 12:9 AMP**

But He has said to me, my grace is sufficient for you. My loving kindness and my mercy are more than enough, always available, regardless of the situation. For my power is being perfected and is completed and shows itself most effectively in your weakness. Therefore, I will all the more gladly boast in my weaknesses so that the power of Christ may completely enfold me and may dwell in me.

## Day 53

What are you worrying about? What is keeping you up at night? What is depressing you? It doesn't matter how big the problem is or how long you have been waiting on God to remove the thing that is worrying you. It is important that you put that heavy worry or burden in God's hands. He cares for you and doesn't like when you worry. If you give that concern to God everyday, it will free your mind and lessen the stress in your life which comes from worrying. You will soon find that you will feel strengthened in your mind and body. That is Our Father sustaining you!

**Psalms 55:22 AMP**

Cast your burden on the Lord, release it and He will sustain and uphold you. He will not allow the righteous to be shaken, slip, fall, fail.

**Day 54**

What are you fearful of? Is that fear stopping you from making a decision? Fear paralyzes but God gives us freedom from anxiety and fear. Being fearful of something, especially the future can come up in your mind during your time in college. "Is this the right major? Will I get a good job when I graduate? Will I ever get married? Will I meet the one on campus? I have to go to the doctor tomorrow and I am afraid to go! Ugh!" May God strengthen you and reassure you that you can trust Him with all of your heart and fears.

**Isaiah 41:10 AMP**

Do not fear anything, for I am with you. Do not be afraid, for I am your God. I will strengthen you. Be assured, I will help you. I will certainly take hold of you with my righteous right hand; a hand of justice, of power, of victory, of salvation.

## Day 55

The physical heart is an organ that is the central point of our body. It is the place that delivers all of what we need to the rest of our body for healthy function. It is the same spiritually. Our heart is the central point and it houses our emotions, will and our conscience. It is the place that motivates our actions. If you are angry, that is an emotion that is in your heart. As a result, you will probably act that emotion of anger out on someone, which can bring about a problem or issue in your life involving that person. So it is with feelings of joy and happiness. If these are the emotions in your heart, you will more than likely be kind and loving towards others. The end result will be positive encounters with others. The condition of your spiritual heart is a direct reflection of your outward character. Therefore, it is important that you keep a good watch over the condition of your spiritual heart. Check it daily to make sure that you are managing your emotions, will and the focus of your mind. Ask God daily and even several times a day to help you to guard your heart from allowing bad things to creep in or remain in your heart that will give life to bad actions and poor character.

**Proverbs 4:23 AMP**

Watch over your heart with all diligence, for from it flows the issues of life.

**Day 56**

**2 Timothy 3:14-15 AMP**

14. But as for you, continue in the things that you have learned and of which you are convinced, holding tightly to the truths, knowing from whom you learned them. 15. And from childhood you have known the sacred writings, Hebrew Scriptures, which are able to give you the wisdom that leads to salvation through faith which is in Christ Jesus; surrendering your entire self to Him and having absolute confidence in His wisdom, power and goodness.

## Day 57

Are you having a difficult time sleeping? Are you consistently staying up late studying and getting up early as well? It is time for you to put in place some new strategies to manage your time better. You should not be consistently losing sleep for studying or anything else. Yes, it is normal for college students to study all night during finals and high stakes exams and papers but it shouldn't become your normal routine. Getting rest is important and healthy. God thinks so as well!

## Psalms 127:2 NKJV

It is vain for you to rise up early, to sit up late; to eat the bread of sorrows. For so He gives His beloved sleep.

**Day 58**

What decision are you afraid to make? There are many things in our lives that can seemingly cause us to be afraid. Fear stops us from moving forward but putting our trust in God helps to remove that fear. Be bold, brave and courageous as you go about your day on campus today!

**Psalms 56:3 AMP**

When I am afraid, I will put my faith and trust in you.

**Day 59**

Our entire doctrine as Christians is based on faith. Everything that we do and believe as Christians is based on having faith. We may not always see God in the same way that the people did in the Bible days but it is still important that we make an effort to trust and rely on God daily. If this is a struggle for you, ask God to help your unbelief in your prayer time. Exercise trusting and relying on God in areas of your life that you normally wouldn't. Enjoy your classes today!

**Hebrews 3:12 AMP**

Take care, brothers and sisters, that there not be in any one of you, a wicked, unbelieving heart which refuses to trust and rely on the Lord; a heart that turns away from the living God.

## Day 60

Mommy and Daddy wounds can be heartbreaking. The love and nurturing care from parents is something that we all need and desire. It is a blessing from God to have good parents in our lives. Sometimes they may make decisions that we don't like but we should honor and appreciate their efforts to be good parents. Of course, as you go away to college it becomes a celebration because you are out of the house and don't have to live by all of those rules. Yes! That can be liberating and quite exciting but try to appreciate your mother and father and continue to do the things that you have been taught that are beneficial to your life, even when you are out of their sight, away at school.

There are students that don't have parents that love them. If you have been rejected or abandoned by your mother or father, this can be a piercing pain in your heart. However, God has promised us that when we just so happen to get a parent or parents like that, He said that He would be there and take their place. That is awesome to know! If you are struggling with the absence of a mother or father in your life for whatever reason, be encouraged that our Father knows all of your needs and will even be a parent to you! May God show Himself as a

Father in your life this week.
Do well in class today!

**Psalms 27:10 AMP**

Although my mother and father have abandoned me, yet the Lord will take me up, adopt me as His child.

## Day 61

Distraction - 1. a thing that prevents someone from giving full attention to something else.

Distraction - 3. extreme agitation of the mind or emotions.

Diversion - an instance of turning something aside from its course.

Deceit - the action or practice of deceiving someone by concealing or misrepresenting the truth.

Here are things that you should look out for as you are on your journey to your destiny: Distraction, Diversion and Deceit. May the plans and purposes of God prevail in your life!

**Proverbs 16:9 ESV**

The heart of man plans his way but the Lord establishes his steps.

## Day 62

It is our obligation as Christians to be watchful and aware of the things that are our weaknesses; things that will tempt us to sin. If you are really in love with your boyfriend and you know that in your heart that you want to have sex with him, it is important that you do not go to his dorm room when you are strongly feeling that way. It is not a matter of avoiding visits at night but avoiding them when you are most vulnerable. To help with avoiding sin, you must make a conscious decision to remove yourself from the source of temptation. Meet him in the caf today!

**Mark 9:43 AMP**

If your hand causes you to stumble and sin, cut it off; that is, remove yourself from the source of temptation. It is better for you to enter life crippled than to have two hands and go into hell, the unquenchable fire.

**Day 63**

**Mark 9:23 AMP**

Jesus said to him, if you can, all things are possible for the one that believes and trusts in me.

## Day 64

It is a great thing when we can believe that God can do the impossible. It is also amazing when we believe what the Bible says and trust that the God that we read about is still a powerful and living God that answers and hears prayers. What are you expecting God to do for you today? If you don't have anything in mind, think of something. Your life is busy and quite demanding as a college student and there are many things that you are in need of. Pray and make your requests known to God with a petition that His will be done as well. Your thought for today is "confidence in God."

**Psalms 27:14 AMP**

Wait for and confidently expect the Lord. Be strong and let your heart take courage. Yes, wait for and confidently expect the Lord.

## Day 65

It is so important that we know the Word of God. Why? There are times when God will not give you what you want when you pray but rather He will answer with a response. If you are not familiar with God's language, that is, His Holy Word, His response will sound foreign to you. So, the next time you keep hearing a scripture or several scriptures, it could be God's response to your prayer! Don't ignore it! You may not always get what you prayed for but a response from God can give you so much peace, love, assurance, direction, protection, comfort, affirmation, counsel and so much more. Even that answer on that test that you just can't figure out! Yup!

**Psalms 119:105 NKJV**

Your word is a lamp unto my feet and a light unto my path.

**Day 66**

Never spend more time scrolling and reading through social media than you do reading your Bible. It is important that you make God your priority daily. Your relationship with God is made stronger by reading His Holy Word and getting to know Him through it. It takes time to discipline yourself but you can do it!

**Psalms 1:2 AMP**

But his delight is in the law of the Lord and on His law; His precepts and teachings, he habitually meditates day and night.

## Day 67

So, you're at the party and everyone is dancing to the music. It's loud and the party is dope! You really needed this party after all of that studying that you did for that last exam! Here comes the drinks!! They are pouring drinks and everyone is taking shots! As a Christian, are you going to take a shot too? Maybe just one?? Should you do it? Everybody looks so cute and grown with their drinks in their hands.

### Proverbs 20:1 AMP

Wine is a mocker; strong drink, a riotous brawler and whoever is intoxicated by it is not wise.

**Day 68**

College is so draining! I have classes all day and then I have to study all night! I just need a break! I'm not going to class today. I hate that Science class anyway! Ugh! I am going to my dorm room and going to sleep! I will catch up on that work next week.  These may be your words as you have become acquainted with classes, professors and College Life. Yes, you probably are tired and are in need of a break! It is ok to miss class for a break or even just to chill. However, make sure you are choosing the right time to miss classes such as lecture only days where there are no reviews, exams, or quizzes being given. You also want to be careful with those professors that penalize for absences. Take your breaks but be wise and watch how much you do it and why. Be mindful of missing many classes just to lay around, watch your favorite episodes or just to sleep because you love your bed. Especially when your roommate is gone. It is so tempting to sleep and lay around in college. There is no one to tell you to get up, go to class or even that you are sleeping too much, but there are still consequences. Excessive breaks from classes or studying can result in you failing a test, a class or even flunking out of college. Be wise and don't love those breaks too much!

**Proverbs 20:13 AMP**

Do not love excessive sleep or you will become poor. Open your eyes so that you can do your work and you will be satisfied with bread.

**Day 69**

Are you the type of person that hates drama with other girls, fighting or even arguing? Or are you the one who is always into it with other girls and are ready to fight or let somebody know quickly? Is there strife amongst you and your friends all of the time? Do you all quarrel/argue often, especially about stupid things? What is strife anyway? Strife is angry or bitter disagreements over basic things. So, what does it mean to quarrel? It also means an angry argument or disagreement, between two people who are usually on good terms. Is this happening in your friendships? It is wise for you to not continue to engage in this type of lifestyle with a friendship. The truth is, those people are actually not your friends. You should not always have disagreements or arguments with those that you call friends.

In cases where the person is not your friend but in certain circles on your campus that may invoke more arguments or even dislike you or the group of girls that you hang out with is another reason to remove yourself and not get caught up in those types of arguments and battles. It is not worth your time, the stress or even your energy. Of course, you can't control who likes or dislikes you, but you can take control over who has your mind and emotions on the matter.

Stay peaceful and be wise in regard to who you call friend and who you decide to consider to be your girls! Yes, there will be disagreements in friendships but it should not be often and outweigh the good times that you spend together. If you are uncomfortable in your friendships, it is time for a change. It is OK to change friends. Don't be pressured to stay in friendships that are unhealthy no matter how long you have considered yourselves to be friends, even if it was in high school or earlier.

**Proverbs 20:3 AMP**

It is an honor for a man to keep away from strife by handling situations with thoughtful foresight but any fool will start a quarrel with no regard for the consequences.

## Day 70

Gossiping is the worst! Right? Why is it that we love to hear juicy gossip? Of course, that is, as long as it is not about us. That girl is so cool but she gossips all the time! Be careful not to become friends with gossiping girls on your campus! If they will tell another person's personal business, they will soon tell your personal business. They may seem very trustworthy and you probably would never think that they would share your secrets but the truth is, their character says otherwise. Gossiping girls usually appear to be very trustworthy but betrayal is always soon to come. Stay away from the gossiping girl and do not make her your friend. She can't be trusted, even though she may tell you that she would never tell anyone your secrets. Watch your gossiping and watch the gossiper! Talking about someone else's personal business may be exciting because you are the first to tell the juicy news to someone that doesn't know but it doesn't feel really good when you are the one that the gossip is about, whether it is true or not. Beware of the gossiper!

### Proverbs 20:19 NIV

A gossip betrays a confidence, so avoid anyone who talks too much.

## Day 71

You will probably encounter professors and even fellow students that may strongly argue in your classes that there is no God. It is important that you know what you believe and why, especially in college. It is probably one of the first places where your beliefs will be challenged. Be confident and know that your God is real. Don't argue in anger but peaceably make your statements when necessary.

### Psalms 53:1 NIV

The fool says in his heart there is no God. They are corrupt and their ways are vile. There is no one who does good.

## Day 72

Your devotional entry from yesterday spoke about what the Bible says about those that say that there is no God. In the next verse, the Bible speaks of those that God seeks. It is very interesting! Do you long for God daily? Do you really desire to spend time with God and read His word before you start your day of classes, exams, club meetings, practices or hanging out with your friends in the caf? Is God and following the Bible an essential part of your life? Don't just read your Bible to say that you read it but seek to understand it and apply it to your life. It is a beautiful thing to desire God's presence and enjoy it. It will only grow stronger as you get older if you make God an essential part of your life. The more time that you spend with God and delighting yourself in His presence, the easier it will become to hear Him as well as understand Him. So, don't be afraid to be called the "Church Girl!"

**Psalms 53:2 AMP**

God has looked down from heaven upon the children of men to see if there is anyone who understands, who seeks after God, who requires Him, who longs for Him as essential to life.

## Day 73

Are you wondering if God hears your prayers? It may sound weird to pray that God hears your prayers but you can! David in the Bible did! It's a simple prayer!

### Psalms 54:2 AMP

Hear my prayer O God and listen to the words of my mouth.

## Day 74

Betrayal by someone that you call friend can be devastating. It can feel as though you have been stabbed in the heart by someone that you thought would never do such a thing. She was your friend and you trusted her! Now, she has betrayed you and you're angry and quite shocked! It is worrying you everyday and you're wondering if you should do something to get back at her, confront her or just brush it off and act like it never happened. The first thing that you should do is ask God for the right attitude to confront her with: one that is of peace and love despite your anger and disappointment. It is a good thing to confront your friend about what she did to you. It is better to express your feelings and get it out instead of letting the hurt sit in your heart and you become the bearer of unforgiveness, vengeance and bitterness. Give all of these concerns and worries to God. After you have confronted your friend with the issue that you have with her, trust that God will ease your mind, give you peace about the matter and strengthen you through this tough issue.

**Psalms 55:20-22 AMP**

20. He, my companion has put out his hands against those that are at peace with him. He has broken his covenant of friendship and loyalty. 21. The words of his mouth were

smoother than butter but his heart was hostile. His words were softer than oil yet they were drawn swords. 22. Cast your burden on the Lord, release it and He will sustain and uphold you. He will never allow the righteous to be shaken, slip, fall, fail.

**Day 75**

We all have this ongoing question. "Did God hear my prayers? I know, well I think that He heard me last time... Did He hear me this time? I pray like all day, everyday. I'm always talking to God!"

**Psalms 55:17 AMP**

Evening and morning and at noon I will complain and murmur and He will hear my voice.

## Day 76

You are out with your friends and a car pulls up. It is sleek and shiny. The car is adorned with sparkling tire rims and loud music. The guys in the car are trying to get you and your friend's attention. You are not sure if you should respond or keep going. They seem like some bad boys. You know! They are probably dope boys. Oh yes! That one on the driver's side is cute, though! What would it hurt if you gave him your number? How he chooses to make his money has nothing to do with you. Right? Besides, he could be a gentleman and treat you well?? Let's take a look at what the Bible says about those who make money dishonestly. In other words, dishonest gain.

**Habakkuk 2:9-10 AMP**

9. Woe, judgement is coming to him who obtains wicked gain for his house and thinks by doing so, to set his nest on high that he may be rescued from the hand of evil. 10. You have devised a shameful thing for your house by cutting off and putting an end to many peoples so you are sinning against your own life, forfeiting it.

**Day 77**

**James 1:22 NIB**

Do not merely listen to the word and deceive yourselves but do what it says.

**Day 78**

There are times, even as young adults, that we have to face sicknesses and scary diagnosis in our lives. It doesn't matter how severe or mild the disease, it is important for you to exercise your faith and believe that God can heal you. This can be difficult to do when you are facing pain and severe diseases that could be life changing according to doctors. No matter the severity and how bad it feels or looks, continue to believe and speak what the Bible says about healing.

**Psalms 103:2-3 NKJV**

2. Bless the Lord O my soul and forget not His benefits. 3. Who forgives all your

iniquities, who heals all your diseases.

## Day 79

"It is really hard for me to believe that God can heal me of this disease." These could be your words as you face reality. It is normal to feel that way sometimes, especially when you may be dealing with a sickness that is incurable or the outcome doesn't look good. It can really cause your faith to decrease. However, when you are feeling this way, it is important that you pray and ask God to help your unbelief. Remain honest with God about your inner most feelings regarding the matter.

### Mark 9:24 NLT

Immediately the boy's father exclaimed. I do believe; help me to overcome my unbelief.

**Day 80**

You are in your first semester of college and the credit card offers are dropping in your mailbox! It is quite flattering to receive and is a sign that you are really an adult. Be careful in signing for those credit cards! It is very easy to accept and start using immediately. It feels so right. You can now go shopping on your own without asking anyone for money. You can shop, shop, shop and no one can say anything. It is your name and responsibility. Right?? Yes and absolutely! So, it is important that you choose which credit cards and how many you will sign up for and accept. Remember, you are now establishing credit and it is very easy to build it well at this point in your life or things can go really bad regarding your credit if you do not pay your bills on time. Do not commit to any credit cards or make purchases that you can't afford to pay back on time. Your credit and your good name are important. It speaks to your character and life disciplines on paper. Don't forget, you will eventually want to buy a new car, house, establish a business and so much more. A good and trustworthy name is needed for that!

### Proverbs 22:1 AMP

A good name earned by honorable behavior, Godly

wisdom, moral courage and personal integrity is more desirable than great riches and favor is better than silver and gold.

## Day 81

So, your boyfriend has a quick temper, huh? He gets angry so fast and you try not to do anything to make him angry. Do you get nervous when he acts like that? Deep down inside, you feel like he may hit you but then again, he loves you. He would never hit you. Right?? Be honest with yourself and don't ignore the signs of an angry undisciplined guy. Your feelings and his actions are signs of an abusive relationship in the making. Do not stay in a relationship with a guy like that. Do not let love blind you and cause you to not make wise decisions about your life. Get out of that relationship as soon as possible! You are headed in the wrong direction! You can always get a new boyfriend, not a new life. Maybe this does not apply to you but you may have friends with boyfriends who treat them this way and you are noticing the signs. Be a good friend and say something to her about your observations and concerns. Good friends don't let their friends stay in abusive relationships! She may deny it in the beginning but don't let up. Keep expressing your concerns to her!

Proverbs 22:24-25 AMP

24. Do not even associate with a man given to angry outburst or go along with a hot tempered man. 25. Or you will

learn his undisciplined ways
and get yourself trapped in a
situation of which it is hard to
escape.

## Day 82

You've made it to the end of your first semester in college, practically! However, that major you chose is not what you expected. You want to change your major, like right now. You have a new major in mind. Maybe two or even three options. You are so undecided right now. Changing majors is a big step and it is important that you do not make quick decisions, especially if you are changing majors because of difficulties in a particular class. College is difficult and will become more challenging as you move forward in any major. It is vital that you choose a major that not only yields a great salary but also equips you with tangible skills that you can use when you graduate. It is better for you to work hard in a major and enjoy the benefits of the salary and lifestyle that it will provide you in the end rather than giving up on a major that is challenging in exchange for a major that is easy but yields a low salary and no skills after graduation, just theory.

If you are absolutely wanting to change your major, the best thing to do is pray and ask God to give you wisdom as you make your decision. Be sure to schedule an appointment with your Academic Advisor to receive professional feedback on your potential new majors. Do not change your major without praying first and seeking professional counseling from your advisor. Changing majors is major and can have adverse effects on your future if chosen without using wisdom.

**James 1:5-6 AMP**

5. If anyone lacks wisdom to guide him through a decision or circumstance, he is to ask of our benevolent God who gives to everyone generously and without rebuke or blame and it will be given to you. 6. But he must ask for wisdom in faith without doubting God's willingness to help; for the one who doubts is like a billowing surge of the sea, that is blown about and tossed by the wind.

## Day 83

There are special spiritual gifts that God gives us to help others in a variety of ways. Spiritual gifts are an honor to have and bring glory to God when used. They are like these superpowers for believers given by God. As you mature as a Christian, it is important that you dedicate the time to discovering the spiritual gifts that God has given you. A good resource is Discover Your Spiritual Gifts by C. Peter Wagner. There is also a Spiritual Gifts questionnaire that you can take to help you to narrow down your Top Gifts. The questionnaire is by the same author entitled Finding Your Spiritual Gifts

Questionnaire. Happy Discovery!

**Romans 12:6-8 AMP**

6. Since we have gifts that differ according to the grace that is given to us each of us is to use them accordingly: if someone has the gift of prophecy, let him speak a new message from God to His people in proportion to the Faith possessed. 7. Of service, in the act of serving or he Who teaches, in the act of teaching. 8. Or he Who encourages, in the act of encouragement. He who gives with generosity. He who leads with diligence. He who shows mercy in caring for others with cheerfulness.

**Day 84**

**Psalms 119:11 NKJV**

Your Word have I hid in my heart that I may not sin against you.

## Day 85

Are you staying in contact with your church while you are away at college? It is important that you continue to attend church even if it is through livestream? As Christians, our faith is increases when we hear our spiritual leaders speak. We receive instruction, guidance, encouragement, correction and so much more based on the Word of God. Don't disconnect from your church. It is essential to your spiritual growth, strength and discipline.

### Romans 10:14 NIV

How can they call on the one they have not believed in; and how can they believe in the one of whom they have not heard and how can they hear without someone preaching to them?

**Day 86**

It is important that you always posture yourself in a place to hear the Bible taught and preached.

**Romans 10:17 NKJV**

So then, faith comes by hearing and hearing by the word of God.

## Day 87

Are you ashamed of being a Christian? Do you feel like the boring girl in the crew? You don't smoke, drink, party like crazy, dress provocative like the other girls and God knows that you are trying your best to not have sex with your boyfriend! Is it starting to seem like the good girl thing is getting boring and making you an outcast? Don't be ashamed. Continue to strive daily to live a Holy lifestyle. It may not always be the popular thing and doing the opposite can be quite tempting but being in right relationship with God is rewarding. It gives you so much peace when you know that you are in right standing with God as opposed to ducking and dodging God for what you did last night. Keep being you and do not be afraid to stand out as the Church Girl.

**Romans 10:11 NIV**

Scripture says, anyone that believes in Him shall not be put to shame.

Day 88

Are you having a difficult time choosing a church home? You are no longer a child and you want to go to a new church. You feel like it is time for a change. The church that you grew up in is not doing anything for you anymore. So, how are you going to pick a new church? Of course, we all have our preferences based on familiarity, upbringing and even current trends. However, in choosing a new church, there is one main component amongst others that must be present. That is, the presence of God. You should experience tangible and or visual demonstrations of God's power in a potential church home. Pray and ask God for direction as you make this big decision. It is ok to leave your childhood church! Happy searching!

**1 Corinthians 2:4 NIV**

My message and my preaching were not with wise and persuasive words but with a demonstration of the Spirit's power.

## Day 89

Have you ever wondered why at some churches people stand randomly, they lift their hands and even bow? These are signs of praise, worship, reverence and submission to God. It is important that you understand why you do the things that you do at church and not just do them by habit or ritual. It is ok to get understanding in the things that may seem quite obvious and understood.

### Nehemiah 8:5-6 NIV

5. Ezra opened the book, all the people could see him because he was standing above them and as he opened it, the people all stood up. 6. Ezra praised the Lord, the great God and all the people

lifted their hands and responded, Amen, Amen; then they bowed down and worshipped the Lord with their faces to the ground.

## Day 90

"I think that I have the Holy Spirit with the evidence of speaking in tongues? Sometimes I am not sure because I don't sound like other anointed people. What am I speaking in tongues for anyway?"

Are these some of your thoughts about speaking in tongues? Everyone's tongues should sound different. It is unique to you and a gift given by God. Just as your natural voice is distinct, so is your spiritual language. You do not have to compare your tongues to others around you. Embrace the gift and be confident. Praying in tongues helps you to build yourself up in the spirit. If you are feeling weak in your flesh and temptations are strong, pray in tongues to get more spiritual strength!

**1 Corinthians 14:4 NIV**

Anyone that speaks in a tongue edifies themselves but the one who prophesies, edifies the church.

**Day 91**

**1 Corinthians 14:14-15 NIV**

14. For if I pray in a tongue my spirit prays but my mind is unfruitful. 15. So what shall I do? I will pray with my spirit but I will also pray with my understanding. I Will sing with my spirit but I will also sing with my understanding.

**Day 92**

There is something precious about being unmarried. The best thing that you can do before marriage is use your time wisely by investing in yourself, your academic and career goals and your relationship with God. It is important to have a clear understanding of the call of God on your life and its requirements before you enter into a serious relationship that will more than likely lead to marriage. The purpose and plans that God has for your life play an intricate role in who you decide to marry. The person must be compatible for who you will become not who you currently are at this time in your life. Therefore, it is extremely important that you discover who you are, some portions of God's plans for you and clarity on your personal/future goals before you decide to date a guy that is potentially incompatible to who you will become. Be careful not to be so consumed with becoming someone's wife that you miss the opportunity to develop into the young lady that God has purposed you to be. Date with caution. Keep your relationship with God as your number one priority.

**1 Corinthians 7:34-35 NIV**

34. And his interests are divided; an unmarried woman or virgin is concerned about the Lord's affairs. Her aim is to be devoted to the Lord in both

body and spirit but a married woman is concerned about the affairs of this world, how she may please her husband. 35. I am saying this for your own good, not to restrict you but that you may live in a right way, an undivided devotion to the Lord.

**Day 93**

That guy on campus is so fine! Every time that you see him, it just does something to you. You want to say something to him so bad but you just can't find the words. You see him almost everyday after class walking into the caf. You look but you try not to stare. Ooh, he is so cute. You wonder, what would life on campus be like if you were his girl? Your desire is growing stronger for him as you continue to see him in the hallways day after day. You all finally bump into each other and he decides to spark a conversation and say hello. You are so mesmerized by his looks that you are not really thinking straight. He is doing most of the talking and you are just answering his questions. After you all have a quick conversation, you think about it and realize that you didn't get a chance to ask him any of the questions that you would normally ask a guy when first meeting him.

Be careful in the initial dating process that you do not become so mesmerized by the looks of a guy that you stop thinking and making wise decisions. Pay close attention and be careful that your desires do not cause you to make quick, unwise decisions in your dating processes. Be bold and confident. Ask pertinent questions about the guy that you need to know to make proper decisions in regard to moving forward with dating or even getting to know him.

**Proverbs 19:2 NIV**

Desire without knowledge is not good. How much more will hasty feet miss the way.

**Day 94**

So, you are in the "getting to know him" process. It is obvious that you wouldn't date a guy that wasn't a Christian. However, this guy is saved but you notice that while he attends church every Sunday, he also goes to the club every Friday and Saturday. You don't like the club and partying is not your thing. He wants you to go with him to the club but you just don't feel right about it. It's just not the way that you want to live your life as a Christian. You also notice that he reads his Bible when things get difficult but not every day. It seems like he only draws close to God when he is in trouble or in need of an answer from God right away. Although he attends church every Sunday, he doesn't really seem to be seeking to find out if God is calling him to do something special for Him. On the other hand, you strive to read your Bible every day. Well, or at least read a scripture to get you going daily so that you can hear what God is saying to you for the day. You are actively seeking to find out what God has purposed for your life. Actually, you kind of feel like there is a prophetic call from God on your life but you are not that sure at this point.

As you can see, the obvious "unequally yoked" is not there, which is the most popular kind; being connected to the unbeliever. However, there is another level of mismatch that you can have with a person that is beyond the surface level of being unequal with believers and unbelievers. In this case, though both of you are believers, the thirst and desire for God and even ways of living as Christians are different. This may not seem as big now but if you continue in the dating relationship and even possible marriage, this mismatch will interfere with your growth and development in God. You will find yourself struggling to be obedient in the things of God because they will be so much more different than the values that you're dating partner has in his life. Just take a look further down the road and think about what life would be like if you were married to someone that does not have the same thirst for God as you do.

Be careful when dating Christian guys. Look deeper to find out how much they are hungering and thirsting for God and his righteousness as well as paying close attention to their lifestyle. It is always a plus to date a guy that loves God more than you and desires his presence, to be in right standing with Him and seeks to be obedient to God more than pleasing his flesh or you.

**2 Corinthians 6:14 AMP**

Do not be unequally bound together with unbelievers. Do not make mismatched alliances with them, and consistent with your faith. For what partnership can righteousness have with lawlessness or what fellowship can light have with darkness?

## Day 95

Life can get tough and throw some punches your way. It is important that you as a believer always keep in your mind on who your enemy is... It is the devil and he will use people to get his agenda done. Be alert and stay prayerful. Fight in the spirit and not in your flesh. Put on the whole armor of God as mentioned in Ephesians 6. This Scripture teaches you how to fight in the spirit and stop the fiery darts of the enemy. I encourage you to know this scripture well and even place this in your dorm room as a reminder that you must always be watchful and praying in the spirit as well as with understanding.

**Ephesians 6:12 KJV**

For we wrestle not against flesh and blood but against principalities, against powers, against the rulers of the darkness of this world, against spiritual wickedness in high places.

## Day 96

The stress of college and finals can get pretty bad. However, you do not have to let finals and difficult courses get the best of you. It is important that you properly plan and discipline yourself for the rigors of finals. It is important that you dedicate the appropriate time to each subject as well as scheduling out your study over a period of time so that you are not caught cramming for a final exam. It is important that you put forth all of your effort into studying which is the only way that you can ensure that you will get a great grade as an end result. Be careful that you do not let the work study time of finals pile up on you. Watch the laziness that can creep up on you because of the overwhelming feelings of failure and success. Remain diligent, positive and study hard for every final that presents itself. Pray before every exam and ask God to bring to your remembrance anything that you studied but can possibly forget while taking that exam. It is your responsibility to be diligent and study by properly preparing for your exams instead of relying on God to miraculously give you answers to the questions that you don't know. Work hard, study hard! Do everything with your best efforts!

**Proverbs 13:4 AMP**

The sole appetite of a lazy person craves and gets nothing, for lethargy overcomes ambition but the sole appetite of the diligent, who works willingly is rich and abundantly supplied.

## Day 97

Oh! This is just a friendly reminder that Christian girls don't date married men. It doesn't matter how good looking he is, his charm, how he makes you laugh or feel or the promises that he has made you. Do not fall into that trap of sin. It doesn't matter how lonely you are, be sure to make the right decision. The decision that your Father God would be pleased with!

### Hebrews 13:4 NIV

Marriage should be honored by all and the marriage bed kept pure. For God will judge the adulterer and the sexually immoral.

**Day 98**

Oh! One more thing! Christian girls do not date or experiment with those of the same sex! It doesn't matter how popular it is to date other girls or experiment with kissing or doing other things with girls in your dorm room, it is not acceptable in the eyes of the Lord. Keep this in mind as you journey through your undergraduate time on campus. It is important that you do not fall into the temptations of what is popular and trendy. Be mindful to stay away from girls who may call themselves your friends but will try to provoke you to experiment or date other girls. They are leading you into sin. Friends do not lead friends into sin! Be watchful of even the smallest signs of the spirit of homosexuality trying to creep into your life. Stay watchful, be alert and always pray for God to give you wisdom as you go through friendships, scenarios and all that college life presents your way that you may remain in right relationship with our Father.

**1 Timothy 1:9-10 NIV**

9. We also know that the law is made not for the righteous but for law breakers and rebels, the ungodly and sinful, the unholy and irreligious, for those that kill their mothers or fathers, for murderers. 10. For the sexually immoral, for those practicing homosexuality, for

slave traders, liars and perjurers and for whatever else is contrary to sound doctrine.

## Day 99

Dorm life is amazing when you are in a relationship. There are very few people around to tell you what to do. You can stay in your boyfriend's room as much as you want. You love him and spending the night with him feels so good. You all seem so much closer since you started sleeping together. Oops! You're not sleeping with him, just sleeping with him. Be careful of the tempting situations that you allow yourself to be put in. Dorm night outs with your boyfriend can be the most tempting situations for the most holy of Christians. The truth is, you will have those nights where you want to spend them with your boyfriend and you will act on it and stay with him. However, it is important that you pay close attention to your desires and recognize when you are weak so that you can make good decisions in regard to when it is just not a good night for you to stay in an effort to remain pure and not sin.

Is it difficult to not want to fornicate on your college campus? Yes and absolutely! So, it is your responsibility to manage your desires within your relationship very well. If you are feeling hot, do not go to his room that afternoon, morning or night! Stay away until you cool down and gain strength! If you make a mistake and sleep with him, repent and move forward. Do not condemn yourself after you have asked God for forgiveness. Keep in mind that once you start having sex, especially with someone that you love, it is very difficult to stop, regardless of how strong or holy you may feel. You will appreciate remaining a virgin until marriage, even though it may seem like it is far, far away from your life now. Your husband will appreciate it also. It is a wonderful feeling to be pure and untouched on your wedding night. Keep this in mind as you go through your undergraduate years. Your goal is to remain a virgin until you are married. It is a great goal to accomplish, you will be pleased with yourself, God will be pleased with you and your future husband will be extremely excited! You can do it!

**1 Thessalonians 4:3 KJV**

For this is the will of God, even your sanctification that you should abstain from fornication.

**Day 100**

It is important that you continue to give your tithes and offerings to your church while you are away at college, if you are working. It is a biblical principle that God honors and even has a promise of blessing from God attached to it. It is really easy to keep all of your money from working in your pocket but you must remember that God blessed you with that job. What is 10% when you get to keep the 90%? Be careful that you do not rob God in your tithes and offerings. It is so not worth it. Remember, the 10% does not belong to you, as a Christian. Offering is also a form of worship to God. It is sacred.

**Malachi 3:10 NIV**

Bring the whole tithe into the storehouse that there may be meat in my house. Test me in this, says the Lord Almighty and see if I will not throw open the flood gates of Heaven and pour out so much blessing that there will not be room enough to store it.

**Day 101**

**Numbers 12:6 KJV**

And He said, hear now my words; if there be a Prophet among you, I, the Lord will make myself known unto him in a vision and speak to him in a dream.

**Day 102**

**Proverbs 31:30 NKJV**

Charm is deceitful and beauty is vain but a woman that fears the Lord, she shall be praised.

**Day 103**

**Psalms 62:8 NKJV**

Trust in Him at all times, you people pour out your heart before Him. God is a refuge for us. Selah

## Day 104

Life on campus can become very exciting. There are so many things to choose from that seem so much better than going to church, sitting in your dorm room reading your Bible and turning down parties, fine guys or sorority offers. However, the truth is, many of those things that are socially popular on campus are high risk for a Christian girl because the likelihood of it leading you into sin is very high. Do not be mesmerized at the dopeness of the college parties, the pretty girls in cute colors, drinking to look gorgeous and grown or sleeping in your boyfriend's room all of the time. These things and many more things that go on in the dorms and on campus can be appealing and fulfilling to your flesh. Life outside of it can seem so boring and even depressing. It is important that you choose your social interactions and activities wisely as a Christian girl in college. That one shot that you take at the party could be spiked. The marijuana that you decide to try with your friends in your room could have other mixed in it that causes the frontal lobe of your brain to be altered. The day that you decide to give up your virginity, you get pregnant or herpes. The one night that you take on the dare to kiss a girl in the room, you discover that you kind of like it and now you are struggling with whether you like girls or guys. Or, you decide to join that sorority and soon afterwards it is revealed that you just pledged your life to a Greek or Roman goddess. So, you can afford to say "nah" to the things that seem like it is what's up. Do not let these things make you feel as though your life sucks as a Christian and you'd rather be at the party throwing up shots with your friends in your tight skimpy dress that has all the boys lookin. Do not desire this lifestyle more than the one that is pleasing to God. Do not let your fire for God go out. Do not let doing right become boring to you. Do not lose your excitement for the things that please God. Remember, being a Christian is not a punishment but a lifestyle to be admired.

**Romans 12:11-13 NIV**

11. Never be lacking in zeal but keep your spiritual ferver, serving the Lord. 12. Be joyful in hope, patient in affliction, faithful in prayer. 13. Share with the Lord's people who are in need, practice hospitality.

**Day 105**

What should you look for when you go to church? There are many things that take place in church such as announcements and other formalities. However, you should always be in expectation of experiencing God's power and glory.

**Psalms 63:2 NKJV**

So I have looked for you in the sanctuary to see your power and glory.

## Day 106

If you are a Christian and you have pledged to make something or someone supreme in your life, this is so not cool. God, Our Father reigns supreme in our lives. We don't erect anything in our lives that would be placed in a higher position than the Lord, by our words or actions. If you are a Christian... there is a need for repentance. If you are asked to pledge your heart, mind and strength to something, run hun run! Why? God, Our Father also asks this of you.

### Deuteronomy 6:5 NKJV

You shall love the Lord your God with all your heart, with all your soul and with all your strength.

*Jesus also quotes the above scripture in Matthew 22:37. Check it out!

**Deuteronomy 5:6-7 NLT**

6. I am the Lord your God who rescued you from the land of Egypt, the place of your slavery. 7. You must not have any other god but me.

**Day 107**

If you are a Christian and you give special honor to the Roman goddess, Minerva or attribute the source of your wisdom and Dope ness to her... there is a need for repentance. If you are a Christian. There can only be one God in your life. He gives us all that we need including intelligence and wisdom. Our dopeness comes from God, Our Father. ♡ 🔒 📚

**Deuteronomy 5:6-7 NLT**

6. I am the Lord your God, who rescued you out of Egypt, the place of your slavery. 7. You must not have any other god but me.

**Day 108**

Quoting and learning scriptures by heart are a must for us as Christians. They are weapons against Satan's challenging words to us on a daily basis. However, there is no use in quoting scriptures that you do not understand. It is important that you understand what you are saying. Here is something for you to think about as you go through your classes today; how can you believe the words that you are quoting and you don't understand them? The same strategies that you use to study in class must also be used in studying the Bible.  Strive to comprehend by using additional tools such as a Bible dictionary, concordance and credible commentaries. The dictionary is a go to resource for gaining understanding of words which in turn help you understand what is happening in a sentence and even a paragraph! This strategy is used in studying for class and should be applied to studying the Bible as well. It is more important that you understand it than just quoting it.

**Proverbs 4:7 AMP**

The beginning of wisdom is, get skillful and godly wisdom. It is preeminent! And with all your acquiring, get understanding, actively seek spiritual discernment, mature comprehension and logical interpretation.

**Day 109**

Do not ignore obvious incompatibility with him just to avoid being alone. You already know that you and him are incompatible. Be wise hun.

**Day 110**

Do you remember in high school or elementary school when a person was mad at you or didn't like you for whatever reason? They would show you by not talking to you anymore, blatantly ignoring you or even starting rumors about you to get others to feel the same as them. Well, in actuality, they were probably hurt about something that you said or did to them, in most cases (excluding jealousy because that's another topic). The truth was, their silence was a way to make you pay for the hurt or wrong that they felt that you had done to them. How often are we exemplifying revenge to those that we feel some type of way about for whatever reason by giving them Facebook or Instagram silence? You know, not liking posts intentionally, blocking and unfollowing people without confronting your true matters in your heart. You may not be in high school anymore walking pass them in the hallway, acting as if you don't see them or getting a new group of friends to sit with at the lunch table so that she or he can look stupid sitting at the table alone. However, your revenge has now come out in the form of social media silence. It is still vengeance and is evil. You are making people pay in your own little way. Let's confront our hurts and disappointments more with the person. Vengeance isn't yours. It's really not worth it. Deleting a friend or loved one for unconfronted hurts doesn't solve the problem either. If it is a case of jealousy, it's ok. It's just a time to look inside and deal with why you are feeling some type of way about the fact that they have something that you want. Let's change our hearts. ♡

**Romans 12:17 AMP**
Never repay anyone evil for evil, take thought for what is right and gracious and proper in the sight of everyone.

**Day 111**

Your word is a lamp unto my feet and a light unto my path.
**Psalms 119:105** 💚📚🔒

May God be your counselor and give you the advice and guidance that you need today!

**Day 112**

That moment when you really think about it... you love him but you know in your heart that he still loves her. What's a girl to do? Well, don't ever allow yourself to be the other woman. You deserve better and should not be second to anyone. If you know in your heart that he still loves his ex-girlfriend, take some time away from him and let the story unfold. If he loves you like you love him, he'll come back. Don't wait while he figures it out. Live your life as if he won't come back. Walk away from love triangles.

**Day 113**

God wants you to be completely honest with Him about how you really feel. If you do it, you'll begin to see the walls around your heart towards God start to come down. Where did you stop believing? When did you stop trusting God? God wants to hear from you. He loves you.

www.ingramcontent.com/pod-product-compliance
Lightning Source LLC
Chambersburg PA
CBHW071857290426
44110CB00013B/1188